THE FOUR
HORSEPERSONS
OF A
DISAPPOINTING
APOCALYPSE

GABRIEL WELSCH

PRAISE

Gabriel Welsch's remarkable third collection boisterously offers up a wonderfully imaginative romp through the wilds of pop culture and various amusing suburban conflicts. These poems are at once hilarious and tender in their resolve to praise the very pulse of a busy life—even if we face the knowledge that "loss fires the blood/ loss starts the day, blood fired is the day." In poem after poem, Welsch displays a rare understanding of what it means to reward the reader by uncovering wild, brave, and beautiful truths about the human condition.

—Aimee Nezhukumatathil, author of *Lucky Fish*

Gabriel Welsch's vision is spectacular, even when he's looking at the apparently mundane. Where we might deign just a passing glance (at a paper clip, a salesman at a party, the transcripts of a telemarketer's most dead-end calls) Welsch looks carefully, then looks again. "All I do is look...Looking. Noticing. Eventually every-thing looks back..." claims one of his most endearing personae. Welsch has taken the common details of our lives and "made them treasures," dialing up poetry in the most surprising moments. Deciding not to overlook *The Four Horsepersons of a Disappointing Apocalypse* was "easily the best call I've had all day."

—Camille T. Dungy, author of *Smith Blue*

To Jill—who *still* laughs at my jokes.

And to Karen Craigo—who thought *one* of my jokes funny enough to get *this* ball rolling.

ALSO BY GABRIEL WELSCH

Dirt and All Its Dense Labor

The Death of Flying Things

An Eye Fluent in Gray

THE FOUR
HORSEPERSONS
OF A
DISAPPOINTING
APOCALYPSE

GABRIEL WELSCH

STEEL TOE BOOKS
Bowling Green, Kentucky

ISBN 978-0-9824169-8-3

STEEL TOE BOOKS
Western Kentucky University
Department of English
1906 College Heights Blvd. #11086
Bowling Green, KY 42101-1086
steeltoebooks.com

COVER AND AUTHOR PHOTOGRAPH
Paul Ruby

COVER AND BOOK DESIGN
Molly McCaffrey

STEEL TOE BOOKS is affiliated with Western Kentucky University.

CONTENTS

3. THICKENING

4. SCORCHED EARTH

1. EARLY

wherein

a wheelbarrow • dark rooms invent a new twilight • there are people who just sell paperclips • a mistake you never cared to notice • an uttered prophecy • a bad neighbor • the short-lived dark • litany of the don't call • smiles cut into their faces

THE TELEMARKETER CALLS A MAN
ABOUT A WHEELBARROW

Did you recently purchase a wheelbarrow at our Hackensack store?

It depends.

On what?

So much, really. [laughs]

It's a yes or no, sir, don't you think?

Yes.

To the wheelbarrow?

To the question.

But not to the wheelbarrow, you didn't then, purchase one.

I'm not saying that.

Well, did you or didn't you?

Look. This is just to say—

—what—

that I bought a wheelbarrow. I
used it. It worked,

3

                                                  hauled greens
                                                  to the pile this
                                                  winter, their January green
                                                  fire hot and pure—

thanks, that's all I wanted—

                                                  We're done?
I think. Thank you.

                                                  This is not an ending.

If you say so.

                                                  Hear me out—
                                                  you do not
                                                  know what this precisely
                                                  is, nor why it
                                                  shivers you, bright
                                                  with wrong.

OK.

Thank you.

Bye.

THE TELEMARKETER CALLS THE MERWIN HOUSEHOLD

If you have a few moments, sir,
I'd like to ask you a few questions.

> Wave to me your fires they are nothing

This call may be recorded
for quality assurance.

> The moss burns lightless as snow

Um. Okay. Is there a DVD player
anywhere in the residence?

> The machine gurgles its greed through the forest a great walker

So, yes?

> No

What is the approximate age
of the oldest member
of the household?

> Ash and ash and ash again its thickness its rope its milk

*[. . .you should hear the guy
I have on the line here]*

> I can hear you

I am having a hard time
with your answers, sir.

        I can hear you

I heard you—

        You do not hear

—I just don't understand,
don't *understand* what you're,
you know, saying. I mean,
I understand the words, like,
individually, but when I put them
together, I just don't get them,
I don't grasp your meaning.

        The dark rooms invent a new twilight
        Rancid
        With sweat the mist of the forest here clouds
        And all about the whiff of the humid the dense

This is my job, you know.
I don't need this shit.

        It is your job and it is mine and this
        Rolls less decadent than any words you know
        Repeat it again again to yourself the sound repeating again
        Again promise yourself that you will work to understand
        What you cannot yet hear

Whatever. I assume you'll be
on our Don't-Call List.

Of course I will but only because you decide it the call hopes
sings

THE ANNOYING QUESTIONS FACED AT PARTIES
BY PEOPLE WHO SELL OFFICE SUPPLIES

Yes, there are people who sell just paper clips.

No, I do not travel around in a paper clip van, from office to office.
I don't have a little tray like the candy and cigarette girls
used to wear in theatres. I deal with stores, orders,
or office complexes. Large scale. Not retail.

Usually in the tens of thousands.

Oh, yes, it's the most ridiculously exciting job in the world,
what I always wanted to do. Isn't your job like that?

Well, I guess I prefer staples. But I don't think about it.

Under breath: Why is this so goddamned funny to you?

Not really. I do have a degree, though. History. Yeah,
a liberal arts education is good for this.

As soon as I get a wife, I'll let you know her thoughts on it.
But just so you know, I won't really be with somebody
who cares that much about what I sell or how.

Oh yeah, I sent a notice to the alumni magazine.
Took out an ad in the paper, too. Just like realtors do.
I got bags of mail for weeks.

Oh of course not.

Virgo.

In color, yes. I guess. But I seldom remember them.

No, never about paper clips. Do you dream about law?
Wait. Don't tell me.

Computers have actually made our business soar.

They can't get past deadbolts but I understand
they are hell on diary hasp locks.

Right here in the United States.

APTITUDE TEST

My boss likes to tell how
no one wakes up and says,
that's it. No more law or medicine
for me. Paperclips. That's
what I'll do. No one, at age seven,
has a sales representative
action figure. No one wants
to grow up to sell paper
clips.

I want to say he's wrong.
Now that I do it, I want to feel
like my mistakes and failures
followed some destiny,
not random shortcomings
that left fewer options
year after year.

My two friends took their SATs
drunk, filled in patterns
on personality profiles, sought
the funniest answers. Now
one owns a garage, the other
is a cop. We haven't kept up,
but I know where they live.
I see their cars, their houses,
their wives. I see a lot.

All I do is look. It's what sales

is about. Looking. Noticing.
Eventually everything looks back,
fixing you in the giant
lens of the world you know
you do not live in. You know
you are meant for nothing, you know
all you do is a mistake you never
cared to notice you made.

GRANOLA JONES ENTERTAINS
THE UNEXPECTED SERAPHIM IN HER HOME

Of course his name was Rainer.
He wore his disdain like a pricey wrap.
He didn't look lost, but said he was.
This, he said, fingers a molten flick
to encompass the room, the gesture
accompanied by flutter of chimes
emanating from the innermost part
of her brain and out through her ears,
this is not where I'm supposed to be.

She said, *lie with me,* but it wasn't
some plaintive yelp. This is a woman who
wears Judas Priest t-shirts, who grooves
in a chorus of *yeeeaaahh* anytime SRV
bends a note off the neck of his tele,
the kind of person who roars whenever
Emeril mentions booze or garlic,
someone looking for *boo-yah* in a come on,
and who knows an angel can read the notes
dancing in her blood, knows enough
to pump the right tune, and so the song
dealt in *baby, sugar,* phrasings of Aretha
and Janis, Wendy and Lita, and the flames

of his thighs glossed to leather,
the light of his face roughened to stubble
and teeth, and he folded his hands
in a new prayer at the small of her back.

While she expected every thrust
to be chimes deep in her head,
what rolled in was like surf, and with it
sand that filled her head, bore weight,
and her heard lolled on her neck, a broad
shore of wet sand, where Rainer strode and wielded
a stick to write, there in the wet sand,
oh pure contradiction, joy
of being No-one's sleep

and she would dream of meaning there
for days afterward. But that night, when he finished
and atomized to reappear in the pilled
and sun-faded recliner that had been her mother's,
Rainer lit a Newport, put his feet up, and uttered prophecy:
you will give up your car and not buy another.
You will love a good man and give it up.
You will meet a woman who speaks to the ages
and you will believe in the uncomfortable.
You will put too much tarragon in some dishes.
You will stagger into knowingness
and abandon your smug comforts. You will live
in the shadow and comfort of inaccurate legends,
and you will keep company with people
tormented by ghosts. You will understand me now
but what I say will later make sense only
as an intuition. You will have the power, once,
to set the ground afire. You have no idea.

MR. DISAGREEABLE EMBRACES
THE WHOLE BAD NEIGHBOR THING

BB gun, lawn chair, scarf. And patience.
Then, exploding Christmas lights. Sagging
inflatable snow globes. Their goddamned
dog. Pop and tinkle, pop and hiss,
pop and yelp.

Early mornings, stroll over, hide
the paper. Or just take a section.
Or a page. Clip a single coupon.

Easter Sunday, they sleep late.
Enjoy a shit on their lawn.
A quiet crouch, serene
in that April warmth
and its cool surprise of air
against bare, white-assed flagrance.

In June, flush with whisky started early,
ask *why?*, demand an answer
while the kids next door
pretend not to see the bend
and scowl over the roses.

Why is the usual: *dog barks,*
kids leave junk in my yard,
snow blower drifts, one loud
barbecue too many. Know
just how much can be built

with the Petty Hammer and
the Spite-Forged Nails—
big-assed Leaning Doghouse
of Cranky Froth, surrounded
with drought-tolerant
Fuck You Shrubbery.

When the breeze is right,
when nearly flammable with drink,
hear the ex-wife's voice:
yr a jackass yr a jackass
yr just a mean shithead.
Drinking more won't shut
her up. It'll just push a body
into an ocean of nod,
you bet you bet you bet.

THE TELEVISION MAKES ITS PROMISES
BETWEEN CHANNELS

The dark and quiet, short-lived both,
each a little hang-up, the line's
tiny death. The light stops just enough
to blanket the soup bowl, the afghan's
tatters, the stopped clock, the slide
of magazines to the dusty floor.
As if the pause whispers departure,
the assurance strong as water moving,
that it all leaves for a moment,
before the next blush of car tires,
disemboweled vampires, spinning chickens
over a home cook's electric embers.
Each channel is a call, and you wonder:
is it how we wait for the call, for what might
be there? Or is it how we hang up,
letting the dark, quick and thorough,
promise us the next world,
the one we can't yet see?

THE TELEMARKETER CALLS THE STEVENS OF HARTFORD

Yes, hello, is the main purchaser
of groceries at home?

> The purchaser is not at home. You have not called the
> purchaser of big groceries.

And with whom
am I speaking?

> The sibilant self, stock full with cigars—

We're not . . . really calling
about cigars, sir. We have
an opportunity,
some special coupons.

> so sing a song of genius, theirs to me.

What?

> [the nematodes! They scruffle in my tea.]

Are you still there?

> I am here, anew, tea-freshened and like youth—

[Pause]

> the nature of the consumer increased, heightened.

This is really a bargain. For $39.99,
you get a whole book—

       Put the book upon a hill, and around it all of me

—of coupons, special offers
and bargains from local businesses.

       and behold its quizzical changes, flush with green.

Yeah, heh, green. It will cost,
but if you use it just three times,
it pays for itself. Really.

       Does the self need defend itself in worth
       or coinage bright as eyes, nor slovenly

We're not talking about the self.
We're talking about coupons.

       We always speak of the self, and speak again
       around it, as though a hill dew-freshened
       glancing with shaved books, like twenty hills
       with twenty books—

You want twenty books?

       No.

Any?

Again, no.

Then why?

You among the inchlings, your list, your litany
of the don't call—place us, fire as our tail.

THE PAPER CLIP SALESPERSON ON FASCINATION

When I tell people they remind me
of women, they laugh.
Especially men. *Right, holding tight,*
clingy, clipped, needy. Haw haw.

That's not it at all. I nod,
yes, reassure the smiles
cut into their faces. Turn back
to the comfort of the computer's quiet.

They bend, you see. They curve.
They are strong and smooth, can twist
to do more than it seems they can.
And I can hold them

but they still slip, click
and shuffle into boxes. Funny
how they all look the same,
how I try to bend like them.

2. EXPOSITION

MR. DISAGREEABLE'S LAW OF SUPPLY AND DEMAND

The supply is not of goods. The supply is despair.
The overwhelming supply of despair creates
demand to unburden. My brother tells me
you have that wrong.

Who cares? That's the great thing about some laws. You
make them yourself.

The bells ring, the door a breeze, entry a chime
of demand simply becoming.

> *I have a truck*
> *parked in your alley*
> *overstuffed couch*
> *throw pillows.*

[Direct. Surprising. Usually there's weepiness.]

I'll meet you around back,
but we don't get much
furniture.

> *I don't have much,*
> *just a couch,*
> *maybe some other stuff.*
> *We'll see how it goes.*

[Wedding band, thin, cheap,
skin grown up around it. Hips

wide as a desk job.]

Not sure how much
I can do for a couch. What's
the story?

>My story's made
>of details you hear again
>and again. Enough said?
>How much for a couch?

[Out on the walking trail by the river
women come and go, jog with sweatered
dogs, mace stuffed in their socks. The river
browns by, day-filled, frothed with this city,
shit-deep, peristeronic, noxious, antidote
to anything living on its shores.]

Walk the river. Give me time.

.   .   .   .

Every Thursday, she arrives. She is more than despair,
proof every law has its confirming exception. Every Thursday,
her boxes or bags push in the door, her trunk is left open
in the alley, her belongings bare on a blanket, and she walks
the river, slow against the runners, dun to their bright halters
and tights, soundless to the smack of the feet around her,
more like the river passing below, more like the grey sky
that meets it, invisible like a street, her only refrain how
much how much how much, her voice the dull break of coins,

the whisper of bills, hoarse with cash, a voice nothing
like money.

.   .   .   .

The couch. Thirty bucks.

Fine.

The frames, maybe worth
a buck or two. The art's not
much of anything.

Whatever.

The glasses. Some are chipped.

So chuck 'em.

This is a wedding photo. Nobody
will buy it.

Hang it on the wall.
For atmosphere.

GRANOLA JONES' DADDY

Born under the dusk's first bats, an evening in a field,
as they rivered the humid air over where her mother
had fallen, woodside. Emma Jones had crashed

her daddy's pickup avoiding a deer ghosted from corn—
and had pressed her belly into the prong of wheel.
Stunned womb, and though she ran

her daughter Jewel saw the world field first,
helped into the summer rye by a farmhand who'd answered
the call of what he thought was a wounded lamb.

Dog bay and wing flap, road rush and gravel scar,
she learned her world the way she knows most women do:
blunt end first, then a helping hand

neither foreseen nor earned. And oh—
that hand's surprise at who he helped. How bold his brow,
how fleet his feet, how sudden the dust rising in his wake.

SWEET WILLIAM

The only man I ever met
who didn't terrify me—
not even a bit. My sister
says that's probably the source
of the inertia.

He brought me things—feathers,
interesting rocks, photos of garbage
he thought artful, new words
he'd read, useful tools.

He packed his passenger seat
with things, to prepare
for when my attention
made them treasures.

He told me little: a father
dead, he glad of it. Spare
and melancholy rooms
he never let me visit. A sister
somewhere.

He never said it, but coral
grew through his spine,
ivy at his heart, long grass
behind his eyes—

the reach of his hands
barely more than accident,

his hope to grow over and
disappear by being within.

He is a song I remember
while driving, a matchbook
in the back of a drawer. A dime
in the couch. He is a post card

from any beach, the surf known
and familiar, under a name
you can't pronounce.

WILLIAM HOLTEL IS A NAME IN A YEARBOOK WITH *GREASE*, PRESS BOX, STRATEGY, HAMBURGERS

Four words should not stay with you.
Or one. None, really. Like bad
tattoos. Torn bumper stickers—

how you do *one* thing and it gloms on
to you, flypaper deeds, and you,
sticky with your past.

One thing. *Grease*, Kennicky,
and you're someone's leather
memory. Eat burgers

because your dad says *bulk up*
and you're ground meat. You're small,
so only the press box's number glory

for you. No wonder
reunions die. Only the teenage stars
felt good enough to stay

in town and watch it age
and shift. They felt cocky enough
to stay and fail.

But what's your story? Misery
compelled you to stay for the modest
accident of your life?

The woman next door pawned
all of her furniture one winter,
mad with grief and rage

at the husband who one day
evaporated. You spent months
considering the light at her door,

the ochres and burnt hues
under the crack, wondering
why she didn't pawn the lights,

wondering what she did
in the well-lighted silence
of that empty space,

until you realized one day,
she wondered perhaps about you
and the regimented hours

you keep for the purpose
of routine's bulwark against
nothing, or why

every day, it seemed,
she smells fried meat, onions,
the recycle bin and its weekly

thrust of a ketchup bottle,
folds of sports pages,
trash a sign of what remains.

THE TELEMARKETER BASICALLY ENJOYS TALKING WITH GOLDBARTH, THOUGH IT ENDS TOO SOON FOR HER PREFERENCE

Is the man of the house at home?

> I can't believe you just said that, your throwback euphemism
> drags up a past to lament and praise, supernova twice, bigness
> a narcoleptic paradox running the lice-ridden rungs of time—

—so you're the man, er, the head of the household.

> You could say that.

Excellent. I have some questions?

> Is it excellent? Do you know what you're saying? Or are you
> the loquacious cockatiel, your exuberance a feathered haste,
> chit-chat scattershot like rejected millet flecking a shag carpet.
> We discuss you, you know, over dinner, over grilled fish or
> a burger flame-plump and greasy, while the moon, at once pale
> and thick, opaque as sperm, like turned milk, looks nailed
> to a frail horizon, and we complain, bitch about the everyday
> invasions, grudge and shrug, admit some utility in the cubicled
> greeting mills . . . .

[this is easily the best call I've had all day]

> put up with coy asides and pomegranate
> scatters of salesmanship, of salespersonship, of the multiple
> mutations of commerce, while some of us raise the specter

of a forgotten conquistador who arrived on palm-sotted shores
in 1570, rifle-pricked and steel-cowled, cowed the first native
he saw with a plea for water, for anything other than salt,
anything other than the lexicon of distance and its flat
horizons, and in effect exercised the great prerogative
of free markets, or free enterprise anyway, sans the lovely
parting gifts of affected tele-purchasing by simply getting
to the fucking point and asking, right out there, crackerjack
simple, for exactly the thing he wanted and nothing more.

Okay. We're running a special on appliances.

Don't need any. See ya.

[click]

THE TELEMARKETER CALLS MISS A

May I speak with Kim—

                  Fuck off.

                  [click]

Stare at the screen.

Take off the headset.

Stare again.

Pinch the space between your eyes.

MR. DISAGREEABLE DECIDES NOT TO RANT
ABOUT HOW HE USED TO BE SOMEBODY

He was the original *good with his hands*.
Three minutes and he could have a heart
in his hand, four and he could take a face
right off the bones. Shave a muscle,

slap and cut a vein, shift a wrestler's abs
to have at his intestines. He couldn't suture
speech, clamp a rumor, stanch the drip
of glances that cut as sure as enemies.

Now this parade of piss-ants. Scuff and slink
of the cheap and desperate. A handgun,
a string of pearls, every engagement ring
fondled as if it were the first ever handed

to a pawnbroker. Every cheap set of dishes
where hope and prayer works to elevate age
to the virtue of cash. He is Pilate in the eyes
of every martyr coming through the door,

and Shylock for every vulture with a van
and a booth at some flea market. He works
to sell one knife per day, one piece of cutlery
as a matter of principle. But this woman,

with the eyes not so much dead as beyond,
a gaze stuck in between walls, as if her sight
walks amid voices, this woman does not pawn

so much as resign, as if giving her life

to his care, as if to sell is then his burden.
*You cannot add to my burden. Mine is weight
enough, barbed with its insistence, slick
with its old, old threat. Exposure*

*cuts in and out. Don't look at me like I keep
the doorway to the dead. I haven't been there.
I have been here, always. Rooted in my now.
Pain lives here, its roots in a past I relive*

*and choose to keep from you and all
who tramp in here, tramp in my head. Give
me your damned pictures, your lamps,
your jewelry. Give me the rooms you own.*

*I'll give you the stare in return, the quick
slip of numbers that add up to less than worth,
the appraisal of only what is offered. I won't
give you anything of mine, not even breath.*

GRANOLA JONES GIVES UP HER CAR
AND DOES NOT BUY ANOTHER

Honda Civic, nearly 150,000 miles,
dog hair in the air vents, dog hair on the seat backs,
you know how it is, a couple new tires, no rust,
but the chrome trim mostly gone. Still—runs well!

> *You're not very good at this.*
> *And it's always RUNS GOOD.*
> *Mention oil changes. You got*
> *oil changes, right?*

Sure, sure. Oil changes. What?
Add "regular oil changes?" What else?

> *Lose the dog hair. Get it*
> *detailed.*

Doesn't that cost a boatload? I mean,
I'm not going to repaint this thing,
and I sure as hell will not get stripes
put on it.

> *Detailed means CLEANED.*
> *You'll want it clean so people*
> *Can test drive it.*

Can you just handle this?

> *Lady, I can do whatever,*

as long as you understand
there is a cost. It all has a cost.

I'll pay it.

I don't think you get it.
The car's not worth that much.

To someone who needs passage,
someone who needs to go,
it will be worth everything.

You need to get over your thinking
that you get to determine value.

My mother named me Granola.
I've gotten over worse.
And besides—that's not
what I'm saying.

What you're saying doesn't matter.
It's what you're doing. Clean
the car, vacuum the seats, do
what needs to be done.

. . . .

William goes through a dozen Q-tips
just working the dash vents. Dog hair
tufts the black wool of the vacuum
attachment. The sun warms the car,
the new black tar on the parking lot,

so they sweat in April cleaning the car
for someone she imagines is glad
for the liberation born in turning a key
in a car, in a new lock, in starting
something. William speaks little,
focused on the small work he takes
a task at a time. When she hoses
the car down for the last time,
she hopes it washes the gaze
of the pawnbroker from the dingy
steel, his look a curse on things
given in vain.

William is looking away from the car,
to a short woman, bent at the shoulders,
at her uneasy gait toward the building.
Her story in thin grocery bags, her
voice the weight that bends her shoulders.
A voice William knows, that Granola knows
holds the world in a prism of sound,
and that the maker of the voice has
no idea. William's hands flex into fists
at his side, and Granola knows time
will race for him now.

. . . .

Good job. This will work.
It looks like somebody owned it
who gave a shit.

Your approval means

3 8

the world to me, of course.

Mmm hmmm. You need
another car?

Why? I'm not going anywhere
for now.

WILLIAM SPENDS A WEEK WITH DEAR OLD DAD

I. Something is Going on When the Wall Starts to Bubble

It has to be really hot for wood to melt.
But that's what it looks like, melting wood,
soup made of cheap paneling in an ancient
apartment. When he finally steps through,

your father doesn't recognize you. The hell
or heaven where he was did not prepare
him for anything other than the way he thought
his son would end up. For better or worse,

this wasn't it. A place that smells like burgers,
Goodwill sofa, dress shirts you buy in bulk.
You haven't lifted anything heavy in ten years,
and you can hear him already, on about his back,

how he carried everyone on it for years. But
this figment, this wavering shamble of a man
with a see-through chin and arms of braided smoke,
this pale insignificance in the drab suit

that every dead person on television tends to wear,
minus the gore, minus any evidence of the trauma
of death, or the trauma of his work, the blood
on his hands dried and ground into calluses

on his suggestions of hands, this man just steps
into the room, taking up carpet, the real world

falling into the black hole around him, and even
as a ghost, you thought he'd have more to say.

II. Okay, I'm Not Hamlet, But Come On

This is the fourth night in a row
that you've stumbled out of the wall,
stubbly and blinking like you just
woke up from being dead,
which you must have, because really,
you've been in the ground . . .

> *Why am I HERE?*

. . . for a good ten years, and I barely
know what to say, even though
I've had four days to think about it
after ten years of fantasizing about it
and that one year of going to Stella
about it and almost going on medication.

> *What are you on about?*

This. *This.* I mean, you, here, in the flesh,
I think.

> *Don't poke me.*

I'm sorry. No, wait. I'm not sorry.
You are the one who's here and shouldn't be.
At all. You shouldn't be. Shouldn't—

I'm sorry.

I don't like this any more than you do.
I have nothing to say. DO you?

[All I can see is a football. It's stupid.
He was more than that, more than
a rotten cliché, more than Old Spice,
that he did wear, yes, but more than
firewood and chores and get a job
and bike riding and, well, oh shit—
it's the same story. It is. It's the same
goddamned story. My father failed me,
failed himself, and did it in the usual
ways, with clean hands and a crisp
bearing and a solid work ethic. He did
it the way everybody does it, without
knowing or going overboard or doing
crazy shit. He did it by living without
thought, without overt concern, with hope
that some kind of love was enough. And
it was too much at the same time.]

I have nothing to say to you.

III. Friday Night's Alright for Fighting

You gotta stop this. You gotta go back—

You know about your sister?

No. What?

I see her much more often.

Like this?

Just like this.

Why?

You don't know?

[Watch his hands. They clench
together, fingers knit, bedside manner.]

In med school, money was tight.

I've heard this, you had to work
two jobs. You must have told me
this a thousand times.

Shut up and listen.

[Blink.]

*We lived in a bad neighborhood, a few
blocks from the hospital. Hookers worked
in the building next to ours. I saw more
than my share of dead people on
sidewalks.*

You were a surgeon. You saw dead

people. You surely made a few people
be dead.

> Your mother was sick all the
> time. We had to feed you kids. Your sister
> was five or six. I used to have to walk
> everywhere with you two. We didn't have
> a car. I'd take you and your sister to the
> library, give your mother a break, you
> bundled up on my back. Sometimes I took
> you to work. One day, just out of the blue,
> a senior surgeon offered me money to
> watch your sister sleep. I was naïve. I said it
> was okay, as long as he didn't touch her,
> and I could stand in the hall outside, door
> open. He paid us a lot of money, kept us
> afloat.

[work to breathe, your lungs
stone like your limbs]

How long did this go on?

> Months.

When did you make him stop?

> I never did.

What happened? Surely he didn't—

He stopped coming one day. Stopped
talking to me, stopped looking at me,
stopped everything. I didn't ask.

How did she know?

She woke up once. I told her he was a
friend. She asked what he was doing. I
told her he knew the tooth fairy. I couldn't
think of anything else. She knew not to
believe me. It was hell getting her to
sleep for a while. Once he stood in the street
for an hour waiting for me to give him the
high sign, and after I let him in, I made him
wait while I threw up.

IV. Reunions Never Quite Satisfy

You know that no matter how long you look
at the wall, your gaze cannot really bore a hole
into the netherworld. Mold, grease, construction
tremors, DUIs and more have tried to cave
that wall, and it is there. Solid as the silence
you can now carve into the answer you crave.
Sit there and demand, *that's it? That's it? Just*
that? You can write *what the fuck* all you want,
but as the old man might remind you, the world
doesn't owe you shit, and certainly not an answer.
You're lucky you got what you did. Most people
go their whole lives without knowing how
their folks sold them out. What bits of their soul

they wrapped in butcher paper and set in the window
to grow warm and moldy. You are a cheese, a chop,
a hunk of wire, a vat of pulp. You are a commodity.
You are currency your parents learned they had
in the slow way a shock can build, day on day,
as a life is shaved down to desperate, as choices
fall away until a thin path is left. You know
that path, lined with wire clips, raveling up
a stair to lonely rooms, to a box in a building
where a woman lives alone with her husband,
her days spent talking to voices as unreal as air,
where you yearn to live as the body to those souls.

THE TELEMARKETER'S HUSBAND, UNEMPLOYED, KILLS TIME IN A CAFÉ, WAITING TO PICK HER UP

A succession of curvaceous housewives
strolls in, drawing with them
creamy visions of afternoon languor
in sparse bedrooms in ranch houses
at the back of drought-stricken lawns—
the unusual which might fit
a day's shadowed caverns.

I sit humbled by them,
how their allure only appears
to those old enough, settled
and no longer twitching
with it, to those still enough
to smell the softness in their shadows.

I imagine how they will move
to the phone when it rings, how
their disappointment at my wife's voice
will ripen, outspoken as an orange. How
I will know some of what they feel.
How a hand cradles time like fruit.

THE TELEMARKETER CALLS A POET SHE'S ACTUALLY HEARD ONCE ON NPR TO TALK TO HIM ABOUT RELIEF FROM THE BURDEN OF HIGH INTEREST CREDIT CARDS

Mr. Collins, I am calling today about an important
opportunity for you to start paying down those high
interest credit cards and get on the road
to good credit.

> I don't have credit card debt. Thank you.

Now wait. I've read your poems,
of your affinity for wine
and bread's pleasures, for candlesticks
and clutches of freesias, your taste for brocade,
your love of solid furniture, your likely
lingerie purchases.

> You know, don't you, not to take poems
> as biography, right? You can't just
> strap them down and beat from them
> the details of a poet's life. You know
> that, right?

So they say. But you also write
what you know, right? Clean out
your attic, describe and collect
what you find there?

> That's part of it.

Then isn't it reasonable market
research to have a look at your work
and deduce you've had contact
with lots of stuff at one point?

> Fair enough. You can assume my valise,
> too, is tooled leather, my books gilt-edged
> and leather as well, my dinners tidy
> opulences, but if I told you, in a slight
> stutter, *soto voce*, that I now had just
> finished a Big Mac and was preparing to
> watch Hannity and Colmes, to ignore the
> trifling sky and the corduroy hours of
> evening, would you frown, want to tousle
> my hair, tell me I'm being silly, ship me to
> bed? Or, are you the moth drawn to this
> flame, the spoon yearning to lie with the
> knife, the bureau drawer yawning to be
> filled with folds of colored socks and
> accidental change?

You have a point, there.

> I usually do. I don't care how many
> condescending titters I hear.

Not from me you don't.

> No. True. Never from you.

3. THICKENING

wherein

the carrots repeat • swallowed by the night • bad behavior in a frayed coat • a little scrotal petting • a hollow engine of crushing silence • doubt and fear avoid one another in the old hotel • the same word on a slate again and again • a push of the plain bursting in monotone • the fat of his thumb • longnecks rubberneck and chew

THE TELEMARKETER TAKES LUNCH

Like a script, the carrots repeat.
Baggie after baggie, they remain.
A constant among constants.

Flip through *Star*, linger at stapled
glamour. Calculate the hours
of work to earn a single celebrity bauble.

Open Diet Coke. Consider the chafe
against your fingernail, wonder at your print
and what it would tell, of what has not

healed from last week's paper cut. Once,
you would never have guessed at the volume
of paper this job would require. Once,

you would never have hoped
for a worm of pain in your bones that might
with any luck, pay for the lost hours—

redeem time with insurance. You wish
for a counter, a spray of crumbs, a knife
left there, glazed with the old green

of mayonnaise, a television somewhere
demanding little more than openness,
little more than nothing. You think

how nothing can be sweet.

WILLIAM WATCHES THE TELEMARKETER

If she walked with more haste,
or moved like she meant it, or did anything
to look like she wanted something,
I wouldn't watch her.

But her automatic steps,
grocery heft banging at her legs,
the shuffle there. Every few weeks
her hair color changes, amber

to chestnut to umber with highlights,
while the cut stays the same, curled in
at her chin, just above the scarf
wound at her neck.

I wait for her to want
something. For a want as simple as paper,
or dark as ash, for some sign
in her step or the bend of her arm—

some way with her words, an ache
in a voice I've not yet heard
except through the wall, late,
a word at a time, padded and swallowed

by the night and the building
enclosing our rooms. That voice
is not hers. It is not the one she saves.
She uses it with her husband, or

on the phone with someone she knows.
And it is not the one she is paid to use.
I want to hear the voice she uses
when alone, when she has no idea

of me behind a wall, or on the sidewalk,
or by the river as she walks there,
same steps, same scarf, same efficiency
of hair, same expression, save

for what she repeats to herself,
words I cannot hear yet.

MR. DISAGREEABLE WINS FRIENDS
AND INFLUENCES PEOPLE

He knows the men there
want to say what he does—
so he vents at her who he later calls
the Smug Harridan in the calico dress:

He was all bad behavior in a frayed coat,
smokes on the back porch, dirty jokes
til Calico meeked out, shrewing
for boyfriend, nearby in a polo, beer

held behind his back. *Aren't you
driving?* She's near him.
No men look at him. Mr. D throws out:
It's one beer. Lighten up.

She will use words like *inappropriate*,
when he knows she means
asshole. She'll think 'patriarchy'
or 'macho' but she's old enough
to know better. She'll hate

how language will fail her.
He'll delight in his choices:
*harpie, shrew, bitch, fuckwit, assbag,
hag,* and then: *feminazi,* the one
they really like. He knows it's not fair—

all that ease created by focused hardship.

He's heard it all from The Ex. Knows the story.
But here's the thing: he loves the story.
It's all he has. And he looks at each man

near him, and they know it, too.
Those words link arms in their minds
and dance, all kilts and beer mugs and *nyah nyah!*
in a hairy-legged chorus line

echoing on a stage in an empty theater
where, even though it's free and easy,
nobody goes there.

MR. DISAGREEABLE PUSHES THE LIMITS
OF INAPPROPRIATE BEHAVIOR

Say you're in a meeting, and for the seventeenth time this year, the banker and your lawyer and a bunch of random cronies of each discuss the New Way We Will Do Things. It looks a lot like the last New Way We Were To Have Done Things. So you muse on the options:

—Sit there and take it, like the new guy in prison.
—Fart as loud as you can, assuming you can.
—Say SHUT THE FUCK UP and throw your Evian bottle at the banker.
—Jump up on the table and deposit a turd on the banker's laptop.
—Draw mean pictures in your tablet.
—If she is female, comment on the banker's rack and/or squeeze a boob if you are near enough. If he is male, insinuate that his package would not cost much to ship, if he gets your meaning, and if close enough (why not?) give him a little scrotal petting.
—Build a stockpile of silent resentment that will, after prolonged medication and crippling bills, kill you.
—Test your limits, the banker's limits, hell, *everyone's* limits.

Suppose you stand as the banker is talking. Suppose you whip your travel mug at the window. Suppose it's not tempered glass (it's an old building) and so it cracks, if not breaks. Everyone's sphincter tightens, while yours feels suddenly loose. The banker makes a perfect oral O of consternation. You say very slowly, while worrying you will shit yourself or develop a flagrant erection or both, "THAT IS THE DUMBEST FUCKING THING I HAVE EVER HEARD, WHICH IS SAYING SOMETHING, BECAUSE WHAT

YOU SAID AT THE LAST MEETING WAS, UNTIL NOW, THE DUMBEST FUCKING THING I HAD EVER HEARD. SO YOU CAN BE HAPPY YOU'RE IMPROVING." You fart very loudly then. And it's juicy. You are mildly worried about your undergarments. Other than that, you feel like a million bucks. You tell the director, GO FUCK A SHOE.

The banker will respond that you are being inappropriate. The banker will tell you to leave.

You love that word, *inappropriate. Inappropriate* is the wrong fork, is writing in a book you don't own, is talking in a theater, is wearing jeans and a chambray shirt when the invitation clearly said business casual. Inappropriate is not being a complete hazardous dick and making people feel threatened. It is inappropriate to use such a word in such a way. It's like putting the American flag on bumper stickers and lapel pins or putting God on a billboard. You want to hold forth on how language is now a failure as we homogenize expression, and then realize that because you are standing and committing what amounts to assault, you do not have an audience ready to discuss with you the finer points of connotative and denotative meaning.

Climb down from the table. You know your life has been a series of *there's-more-to-it-than-that*, that every explanation you've offered has waved the *it's-a-long-story* flag from high on the mast of your rationale. Or something. Metaphor's not your strong suit. So climb down, shake off the silence of the room. Cough a little. Wait for somebody to say something. You know how this goes. The day will proceed. For some, you will be the best story they will bring home to the wife all week. You are someone's therapy discussion, someone's scotch on the way home, someone's desperate grab of her children as she walks in the door. You are everybody's bad day. Your own worst enemy. But the day will proceed. Sure, a cop might help you leave the building, but it's not like that hasn't happened before. Start the car, consider your credit, the mounting bills. You traffic in enough handguns that there's always a way out of this. But that's not your style.

GRANOLA JONES AND THE TELEMARKETER
MEET IN THE HALL

Most days start with blood.
The diabetic in the apartment
across from me trembles in a housecoat
on her balcony, pricking what is
that day her least callused fingertip.
She packs herbs in wax paper sachets
for her son, a priest, who gives them
to the women of his parish. This, too,
she does on her balcony, under
the watching eye of God.

Or so she says. Next to her
a man her age spends most afternoons
obscured partly by cherry pipe smoke.
When his daughters visit, I often hear
them scold him, their voices tearing
the screen door, bright raptors in the dark
kitchen, rattling in the cinderblock
garden of sand between my wing
and theirs. Above those two

are the scholars, two young men
with hunches built with the weight
of books, though they are stout. They
eat poorly and, while I like to think
it is against my nature, I want to cook
for them, something reasonable, a meal
that would make sense to them, one

not uniform in its oily grey, its salted
pull, one not simply filling and forgettable.
They rise early, their windows gold
and thrashing with silent shadows.

In the hall, retrieving my paper,
most days I meet the teacher, bristling
with a riot of red hair and beard and the chaos
of an apartment he shares with his wife
and their new twin girls. Near to bursting,
he bustles, and his broad hands hold
a briefcase like a book, and I wonder
how children get under those hands,
how he holds chalk without crushing it,
how the board doesn't warp at his
gravity, how he lives through the cries
I hear at all hours, how he lifts those infants
and in daylight wears the morning
like a dream of happiness he wove himself.

And for all of it, our building is still—
with windows and rooms I do not know,
and when I think about what happens here,
what lives age these rooms, the urge for sense
rages within me, and powerlessness warms
the rooms, becomes dinner, becomes aspirin
and lint and paperclips that sprout and grow
everywhere. Every syllable overheard
in the walls of this building, becomes a paperclip
looking for meaning in a clasp.

And when I see her, the voice we all here know,
the voice we've all heard after dinner or at noon
or among the channels we watch, she is dark matter,
she absorbs the light of the hall, a moment
bends to her will, and even the walls
bow toward her, the hallway a sudden
roiling tube, a funhouse mirror lined
in cinder block and dull carpet whitened
in a strip in the middle, and her eyes
are rimmed in shadows and ruddy wrinkles,
looking down, where her fingers twitch
tarantella, some sign of the manic bloodstream
of this building's tremor and bustle,
and before I can greet her she says

> Do you hear the voices of this building?
> Do you call them and have them speak
> to you in Sanskrit, or Pashtun, or Farsi,
> or Mandarin, or German, or Gaelic, even
> English broken and pidgin, do they murder
> you in words carved in a tongue, a noise
> not your own? Is your demise written
> somewhere, and does someone describe it
> for you? Everyone here has their story
> written down—did you do it?

I won't write the story until I know the end.
How else do I know what matters?

> The story makes the end, so it all matters.
> You just never know what to say to your own story.

I almost ask how she gathers wisdom
about her like a patterned shawl, the flow
of flowers or filigrees hard to follow,
but I wait and consider a trail of meaning
made in my life only by loss: loss of a man
who helped build the house of my life
and who perished when it burned, or vice
versa. Loss of my womb, loss of my voice
for a year, loss of those with whom I broke
bread or tilled earth, loss of my place
in any of a number of towns, loss I tried
to outrun, loss I have come to find as my own,
the voided font of voice, loss as fuel,
a hollow engine of crushing silence,
wielded against the noise of those who deny
all that loss contains. Loss is articulate,
loss is weighty, loss is this woman,
loss is my body, power and weight,
a voice to batter. Loss fires the blood,
loss starts the day, blood fired is the day.

If she were to stay in the hall long enough,
I now know she would say, you: you
suddenly. You, in loss, know.

THE TELEMARKETER MEANS TO CALL BAKER
ABOUT ERECTILE DYSFUNCTION BUT,
IN A MISDIAL, WINDS UP WITH SIMIC

Good evening, sir. I am calling you
because you asked for more information
about our product, Rigida, the natural
erectile enhancement . . .

                      I didn't do that.

Is this Mr. Baker? *I should have asked that
right away.* So, you're not Mr. Baker?

                      No. Who are you?

[Pause.] Well, that's not really, you know,
important.

                      I know who you are.

If you're not Mr. Baker we can just—

                      You live in two rooms
                      from which you've pawned pictures—
                      their shapes ghost your walls,
                      outlines hanging with no weight.

How do you—?

                      Your laundry seethes at the door.

Glasses fill with spider webs.
You clutch at your eyes sometimes
to remove migraines, to pull them
through your brow like tapeworms.

Who are you?

Sunny Thursdays, your day off,
you pace off the river's bend
in the smell of toast and eggs,
the fry cook's blind sizzle
a shadow scratching your hands.
You wonder where your husband walks
in the daylight, his face euphoric
as a clock.

[weeping—glassine tufts of woe]

You know the taste of air here, don't you?
Sugared with all you lack?
Do the signposts long for clean sheets?
Do the storm grates cough up sweet rinds?

[*Sniffle*] Stop seeing what I see.

Yours is a job for Pilate. Late in life,
after the crust of empire has sloughed off,
when the oranges fold in on themselves,
weighted with gutter frost. Pilate would only
call in the wee hours, when doubt and fear
avoid one another in the old hotel, splashing

their faces with gray water, hands on a chipped
sink as they yearn for the other.

You have too dim a view
of what I do, or the why of it,
that sullen story.

Tell me someone who has a rosy view,
and I'll show you the nail through their foot.

Okay, but who's holding the hammer?

The phone on my card table.
How its legs shake.
How the night rots,
like food at a wake.
When the phone rings, and it is you,
the old men meet in the hall, faces
wet with all they'd wash away,
and in the echo of ringing,
joy creeps under the door.

THE TELEMARKETER'S DREAM

Not work, never that. Usually running.
Or saving people, reaching into deep fear
to curl her fingers at their ears, a final
caress before greater depth pulls.
She whispers to them every new word
she weaves from snippets overheard.

Does she wish the better dream—the one
of a faraway place, of ripe pears in dry plains,
gazelles flickering over sun grass, mind flashing
like trout in a gold river? Or a dream of plenty,
wine, tomatoes, melons, lilies and loaves
and loaves? Or is it subtler, conversation,
pleasant, table-cloth and crystal, or a chenille
couch, a texture of voices and murmurs,
fingers light on the arm?

Or will her husband turn to her one morning
to tell her of his dream, the one she will want?
He sees her in a room with crusts of bread
and a pot of jam. She has no idea what to do
with either. She writes the same word
on a slate again and again. A face ghosts
the window at odd intervals, its brow
a scrawl of furrows. As she writes her word,
her drooping sleeve rubs it out. He breathes
faster, hoping for a glimpse of the word.
She hopes, as does he, to find a prayer.

WILLIAM NOTES THE BOXES IN THE HALL

Would it be too terrible
if her husband has left?
The hall's dusty walls, the wet
cardboard smell, the roughed
carpet and its wear of feet
trudging up and down.

He heard her last week,
a low voice to usher in two men
in coveralls with clipboards.
Their inventory took less
than an hour. What did she think
as she endured the professional
gaze? A sofa goes, then a print,
then an old lamp, then a chest,
squares and ghost tendrils
left, heft of nothing hanging
on empty walls.

He listens for her, wants to hear
her voice bounce off shorn walls.

He does not yet know how one day
he will learn what she does, he will hear
her voice and know that it is her
and not understand why or how he knows.
Her voice: a can, a pillow, a lush
forgetting, a push of the plain bursting
in monotone. How different it will sound

without a wall between them.

For sound, she cardboards, hollows,
dulls like a box. The call? For a warranty,
toaster, good protection. He will have kept
the box, will recite to her long numbers,
will let his finger move slowly
over the receipt, a necessary delay,
even as he wants to read faster,
to hasten her turn to speak.

THE TASTE OF BLOOD

Little more than counter and corners,
twin tables near the back,
the café noises when more
than two people line up
for the plain white tall cups,
all orders the same size,
rowed out on the counter
for every hour's rush.

William comes here between orders,
or after a big contract, or to stop
the creep of numb patches across
his legs. Most days he sees the man
with the round face and the long nose
that he has seen on the stairs
and in the hall, and who lives with her,
a husband maybe.

One day he knows for certain.
He picks out his coffee, forks his bills
toward the cashier, and as he does,
the room blossoms with a quartet
of women in yoga pants with tote bags,
pony-tailed and rushing with chatter
and breath, faint shimmer of sweat.

The man with the happy face
stops the eternal drumming of his fingers
and lets a hand wrap his coffee cup,

anchoring him to a table in this tiny port
where this gentle storm arrives,
and his face brightens while he enjoys
that they do not know how he watches.

Imagine hurling the coffee. Imagine burn
and scald, red cheeks and a leap to his feet.
Imagine the steps back, the swinging bags
and then the quiet while everyone will watch
to see what he will do next. Imagine
the confusion, the man's face a slack
question just before a twist of rage. Imagine
what she will think when she sees

the paper, his face, the address, her knowing
she has seen him. He calms. He smoothes
the lid onto the lip of his cup. The sharp
plastic creases against the fat of his thumb,
then cuts. On reflex, thumb to mouth.
The taste of blood in his mouth. The man
stops watching the women, and turns to William.

GRANOLA JONES COOKS FOR THE POTLUCK

The neighborhood is made of mailboxes
built to mimic the houses they front.
No trees rise over twenty feet. Not one
life exults in a front yard.

Parking won't happen easily. Quiet
in the concentration, wheel rock
on a curb, men with longnecks
rubberneck and chew

in the backyard of blue smoke
and music rising like smog. Meet,
mingle, judge. Meet, mingle,
drift, drink. Mingle, judge. Judge,

drink. Eat a little. Drink more.
Ms. Jones recognizes a woman, Kara,
from the shelter. Her two kids often
watch her husband kick her legs

as she curls and screams on the linoleum.
Jones eats a deviled egg, one she made,
the bite sharp with too much tarragon.
At the smell of a man, her breath

is angel fire, a holy sword at her throat.
She knows at once the shout in her muscles
will pull and ache through her arms later,
the strain of lifting the earth to hold

it against her gaze, torrents of fire
at her bruised back. Kara's husband
puts an egg whole into his mouth,
Ms. Jones knows it will nourish his feet,

and she hears the crack of his jaw
working the egg, as if he can chew
forever, adept at grinding, a master
of breakage, and his kids she now sees

ghosting the swingset hemmed in weeds,
the only children here, their slender legs
a shadow blur when they run or arc
in the swings tethered still to earth,

and Jones wishes Kara her angel
in leather and rage to open her sky
and give her some hope of violence
to burn her square of earth clean.

4. SCORCHED EARTH

wherein

seasonal affective disorder • gift a phone of paper clips
• smell of meat and fire, waste and earth tremor • a silence
plump with the imagined • the scorn electric in this nation
of absolutes • the vomiting sound commences • buried
in eyeliner or sweaters • the twice-baked tater skins are
out and piping hot • mace in a clutch purse for a soccer game •
even your shrubbery wants to flip me off

THE TELEMARKETER CALLS BASHO ABOUT A CURE
FOR THE WINTER BLUES

Good evening, sir. I'm calling today to ask
if you know anything about
seasonal affective disorder.

> Winter seclusion—
> sitting propped against
> the same worn post.

Yeah, sort of. Never
really heard it put that way
before. You're quite, ummm—

> I would like to use
> that scarecrow's tattered clothes
> in this midnight frost.

Yeah, that's sort of it,
too. You see, um, *some* people
when they don't have light—

> Lonely silence,
> a single cicada's cry
> sinking into stone.

Uh, okay, *what?*

> Wet with morning dew
> and splotched with mud, the melon

7 7

                              looks especially cool.

Are you listening
To me? Do you understand?
It's not a day or night . . .

                              Your song caresses
                              the depth of loneliness,
                              O high mountain bird.

Okay, that's enough.

                              Even in Kyoto,
                              how I long for Kyoto
                              when the cuckoo sings.

You think you're so great,
but I can do what you do,
cryptic words. Small breaths.

                              Hmmmph. Your bird flits. Wire
                              to smoked sky, mindless as snow,
                              all sun glare. No weight.

I keep calling poets.
You all do this, throw your words
up like shields at me.

                              Tremble, oh my gravemound,
                              in time my cries will be
                              only this autumn wind.

It's like you don't care
to make sense. Why don't you work
to defend your words?

> Snow's spin-lift, descent
> crush built high with little weights—
> hushed through such chatter.

WILLIAM GIVES THE GIFT OF SCULPTED TELEPHONY

For you, I gift
a phone of paper clips,
handset of stainless runnels,
base row upon row, channeled
wire looping in on itself.

I crouch it at your door.
The cord even winds—
glints, resurrects
the dead light of the hall.

It took hours to build,
hours humming the song
I invented to go with the name
I imagined for you, its lilt
the rhythm of your step.

Lift the set from the cradle
and in the slipping whisper
of catching wire, imagine a voice
on the other end. You do not
have to do the talking.

GRANOLA JONES STAGGERS INTO KNOWINGNESS
AT A SHELTER POTLUCK AND FUNDRAISER

With the telemarketer, she drives to a potluck, a friend she knows
through the shelter, someone else who has ducked knuckles and
packed in the night, once an age ago in another state.

And now she's having a party. And they will go. And William is
there, his body wracked electric and bowed like a divining rod, as
he tries not to meet Granola's gaze while seeking the telemarketer's.
He scoops tabouleh and hummus, bean salad and diamonds of
pita, finds a place on the lawn and looks up, his face a clock of
hope, one eye nailed to the cross the telemarketer bears around the
party. And her husband is not there, is in no one's thoughts save
Granola's. And the pawnbroker, he who has donated to the shelter
every chair he can't sell, a couch he didn't want, dishes too heavy
for his shelves, who has sculpted from his disdain and rejection a
simulacrum of care, eats a small amount and drowns it in wine.
And women wander the lawn, roost in groups, wear black and san-
dals. And their bones press against their skin, all shield and curve
shorn from them, their necks hard as teeth. And as she watches
William drink more beer than he should and as the pawnbroker
gathers with men to flash their hidden smiles near a tree and as the
telemarketer wishes she could speak what is trapped deepest within
her, Granola moves.

She moves into the dull brilliance. She moves among the tilt of
lawn chairs and children spinning around the badminton net. She
smells the men where they gather, long-necked and laughing into
their shirts. She thinks they smell of meat and fire, waste and earth
tremor, and there she finds William, tree-slouched, who on seeing

her pushes his beer behind his back. She says his face is ash, clouds move over his eyes, and around her women stagger bearing the mark of booze, and she wonders why in the hell anyone ever thought it would be a good idea, here, to have coolers iced with bottles. She knows, yes, yes, it happens, people handle it, but here, amid this forest of arms sutured and stitched, where bones bear lines where they knit together again, where every moving limb under skin bears a narrative line where time fractured into loss, here where they have gathered to help, *not here.*

If she could have kept herself from saying something, she would have. If she could have kept spite on a chain, she would have. If she could have carried her world in a bucket, set it under a tree, kept it from pushing what she knows upon everything she sees and does, she would have shown restraint—not for William, not for the despicable and disagreeable bastard by the tree, but for the women who themselves have managed to dismantle the world for a while and dance-step among its pieces. If she could have put the angel and his smart-ass benediction out of her mind, undid his accuracy, his snotty prescience, if she could have pushed past the feel of him, she might not have abandoned herself.

But she does. She gripes at William about his beer, and then he starts, the man with fists like truncheons, fingers like rolls of quarters, knuckles fat and iffy as dice. She considers the hands, the usury there, their ability to lift and take, the flutter of blood, too, in the veins that throb blue across the back of them. She knows, then, though she doesn't understand how, he's never brought the back of his hand against anyone, he's never raised a hand in anger. He's no saint, but his hands, so big, so ready for damage, so thick, have not done their worst. Not yet.

REPETITION

Sales pitches are refrains without a tune.
Her walk drum beats and shakes
him all day long. When he sleeps,
her step is the inhale, her turn the exhale.

Then one day, a ring, a hello, and a question:
*Do you or any other people in your household
subscribe to any periodicals or newspapers?*
Voice of conch shell, voice of tire hiss, voice

like a balm, like an auction call, like a ghost
of his days, like a refrain, drum beat and pipe
organ crescendo landing on a silence plump
with the imagined. His voice inadequate to
describe this voice. He says,

How are you?

Are you there?

Why won't you speak?

        [throat clearing]

*Would it surprise you
to know that I know
who you are?*

No. Not at all.

AFTER CALLING TOO MANY POETS, THE TELEMARKETER GIVES UP

I've tried to speak like them,
with teeth of ash or blood
or some baseless patter,
alone on my balcony,
my voice big as bone—
more deep, more long than on
the phones, its reach a branch
to heaven far from here.

That's not right either.
I've tried their voices, tried
to boost my numbers, tried
to close so many sales
with mystery dressed as theirs.
They have no ears, I've found.
I speak to fleshy heads,
to skin taut where
it should part to listen—
the mind a ready plot
where seeds can slough
their coats and words,
like rain, delight.

I've tried their suit of sound:
ill-fitting, slick-sheened, too tight.

GRANOLA JONES HOLDS FORTH

I'm always amused
at what I'm supposed to understand:

Boys will be boys, but seldom are girls
tolerated unless they become women.
And then they are feared and loathed.

I am to speak only in the defense
of another, and never in praise
of myself. If I sing of myself,
I bear the scorn electric in this nation
of absolutes. I sign what I wear, a mantle
of wormwood and lungwort and bluebells,
harsh with thistle and burdock, furred with mullein.

I am to walk only as tall as expected,
head the height of a kitchen counter or a sofa back,
a headboard or a crib rail, head only as high
as the wool shoulder of a man walking beside.

What I understand bucks in the corral:
wisdom is another word for having patience
to bear the world quietly, and keep doing
what you're doing. Wisdom is no compliment,
no coveted virtue of mine.

Modesty is another word for shut-up, be quiet.

I think these things lightly, in the car,

while walking, while afloat in heavy air
not of my making, in this world inherited
in a field far from things made to endure,
in a field designed to wait the true seed
and its eventual coming, brought into the world
by a man who did not fully understand
what he had done.

I am tired of watching the wages of men
played out in second-hand shops, tired
of watching women load carts with canned fruit
while hollow-eyed children climb the shelves,
of enduring the rusted fenders of cars parked
outside the makeshift shelter in the basement
of the Episcopal church, of finding cigarette butts
and worthless lottery tickets outside the clinic,
of the supremacy of bingo and Kiwanis coffee cups,
of benefits where every volunteer is a thick-armed broad
with failing eyes slumped over a steam table,
and every mother is missing teeth, black-eyed
children, their clothes prismatic grays.

I am tired of those people who waltz
into your life and utter the horrible,
make snide reference to what they think
they know, to the gutpile of insinuation
left behind at a kill site.

So I know, then, what I understand:
walk on, knowing the angel carries your shadow.
Burn when you must burn, render unto

others the fire you have made, and do not wait
for understanding. Look instead to cigarettes,
the lottery, dirt, steam, plastic bags with tubs
of mac-n-cheese, benediction of chewing gum
and antacids, Nyquil sleep and the gut
rumble of Red Bull, beat the body
until beatific, shatter the soul to surly.

MR. DISAGREEABLE FIGHTS WITH THE NOISY NEIGHBORS, THEREBY BECOMING THE NOISIER NEIGHBOR

And so it's come down to this. Scratching
through Web sites for an MP3 of gunshots
or babies crying or vomiting or blackboard
nail scratching or someone disemboweling
a live cat—finding a few, patching together,
running a USB cord into an adapter, an old
stereo amplifier, duct-taping a pair of hoisted
speakers into the window, cranking the volume,
and leaving for a drive.

And still. And still they escalate, their party
spilling over into sirens and red lights a spin
of sequins over the house walls, the faces
now in the street, the live band in the back yard
kicking every beat with a pervasive underhum
and near feedback garnish until a bullhorn
crashes through the noise and before Mr. D
can get to the house the only sound in the air
becomes gunshots at his window, and then
a field of legs and asses prone and weapons
out. The vomiting sound commences. Then
the cat. Then everyone is getting up.

His car is parked, he is out, a whole lot of eyes
have found a place to glare, and he thinks
Pyrrhic victory. The neighbors do not turn
to him, no crowd turns, no thoughts gather
and no notice given, aside from the one cop left

at the house, still writing the citation, still
droning about ordinances, as he finds
he has no taste for the role of the ignored.

She does. The one with the shoes, the one
dissolving her home with each mean handful
of cash he gives her, each transaction a cheat
they both see and yet only he dreams about.
She ignores that, ignores him, talks with words
like grunts, nothing like the cadenced diction
of bankers and cops, the dancing language of law.
Hers the uncaring grunt, the most annoying noise,
the disregard shrieking at him—suddenly all around
in a cloud that is all he hears.

THE TELEMARKETER TAKES A WORKSHOP

The villanelle serves the cycle,
the sonnet the turn. It's all sales.

Chant the bit about despair,
the icicles lingering in a forever fall,
remembered as only potential.

Sing the dog songs, the lapping
thuck of water and the clack of would-be
claws on old linoleum.

Meditate on so many orts of circumstance,
write it and repeat it and take it apart.

Then watch them as they look at you,
so much older, buried in eyeliner or sweaters,
one finger hooked to dial, drumming.

MR. DISAGREEABLE FAILS TO EXERCISE RESTRAINT AT PONDEROSA, ON THE FRIDAY BEFORE A HOME FOOTBALL GAME, BECAUSE HE KNOWS IT'S NO TIME FOR GALLANTRY

As if the doughy matron in the sweatshirt will offer him
that last biscuit or accompanying scoop of sausage gravy.
The frat boys circle like the shadows around their eyes,
and a guy whose wallet is chained to his belt
has a ratchet elbow on his spooning arm and a zeal
that inspires a low-grade, mumbling *DAMN*.
Near the buffet, an infant coughs at his crying
older sister while the parents make the most
of the smoking section. He lacks the urge
to feel better than them, as it would detract
from his focus. A tired woman near the soup kiosk
mutters to herself something about Michelangelo,

coming and going and finally, he stops when
he hears her. Holding aloft a glop of rice and gravy,
he recognizes the shuffle of orthopedic shoes,
the wrist brace, the surprise of her expensive-
looking haircut. She tongs salad, a leaf at a time,
and she mutters again, how the houses are haunted
by white nightgowns, and then he remembers—
the first week, an armload of frames, each worth more
than the pictures or paintings they pinned down.
The next week, four dining room chairs over four
days, she telling him how her hatchback only fit
one chair at a time. She came nearly every day

for months, until she must have emptied her house.

He asked her why once—something he never does.
She winced, and all she said was, "My story's made
of details you hear again and again. Enough said?
How much for a couch?" And here she mutters again,
how hope is the thing with feathers, and then a word
about plums in an icebox, and he wants to ask her
is there something I can do, but hesitates. For one,
he has no wish to be rebuffed again. And another,
the twice-baked tater skins are out and piping hot,
and when having to choose between the two, between
the greasy heat of sustenance and her cold disregard,
it's an easy decision. And besides, he knows that later

he'll think of her, tongue digging the chalky Tums
from the grooves of his molars, the buffet burning
back up into his throat, while he listens to *Performance
Today* in a self-pitying cocoon, staring at the ancient
receiver's mammoth volume button and the electric blue
glow behind it standing in for some spirit crackling
down from the jet stream dialectic roaring over his apartment,
a philosophy made real in radio waves, blue tooth,
cable lines and more, and he will wonder at what words
she takes from it, why what she says, why what she does,
why *she* of all people gets him twitching and thinking like this,
why he remembers the strange things she says. And when
his phone rings he will actually get up, answer the thing,
something he never does, and it is her, and it is something
about snow tires or insurance, and he drops the phone,
clutching at the white arc shocking its way across his chest.

GRANOLA JONES LIVES COMFORTABLY
WITH HER INACCURATE LEGENDS

She tells anyone with a metal spoon
and a glass bowl of the time her sister
banged the rim and later ate a chip
of glass that sliced her throat from tongue
to gullet, and each retelling reaffirms
her rosy view of things: no glass bowls.
If her sister'd speak to her, she'd remind
her: that's not how it went at all. Easier, too,
to think the president had his birth in excess,
among the eternal nod of oil fields, deep
in the hollow of the country shaded in an eloquence
of church awnings and bicycles chained like barnacles
to roadside railings, easy to see only poverty and violence
in the anonymity of windows piled in a stack in project
after project. Or that every woman suffers beneath
the halo some man nailed above her head.

The legend of dirt is its honesty, the legend
of fists is men, the legend of a house
is pain hung on the walls in the tight smiles
of department store portraits. Like a hawk
peering for a twitch of fur, she sees only heat,
misses entire trees. She cannot keep feeling
the stick in her craw and refuse to know it.

For most people, the gap between what
they wish and the way it is favors the cruel.
Ms. Jones sees it slant—men lurking under

hat bills, women pinched under pageboys
with mace in a clutch purse for a soccer game,
corpulent Boy Scouts hunting last bluestems
on a prairie studded with cell towers, killing
a vole or a groundhog or a cat along the way,
bashing it in with a rock, their fists having long
ago learned the swiftest arc to a conclusion.

She hears in my voice a bruise, she telegraphs
my frown for damage. When I talk about my life,
she says I never finish a sentence. That's true—
out loud. My husband, she says, looks better
when made of words. My job, she says, and I know,
fires on empty. But really, it is anything but simple,
anything but the legends she knows too well,
anything but a comfort to either of us.

THE HARRIDAN'S SONG

It's like even your shrubbery
wants to flip me off, like the shaggy maple
by the drive wears a Metal Up Your Ass
t-shirt and biker boots, wallet with a chain.
Your yard wants to kick my ass.

Well go ahead, call the cops. Tell them
how some bitch is here to have a field day
with your lawn ornaments. I'll watch
you finger-part the drapes, I'll watch
how you writhe and leech into your lungs
that diesel smell, that wet sky, that ozone hit,
that engined disaster—the throat
of an intersection—wail at it
and despair. I've parked on your lawn.
I'm here and everywhere—
at your gas station, at your hot
dog stand, at your Little League
game, at your Kiwanis meeting,
at your booster event, at your beck
and guttural, throaty call.
I am the midnight rustlings of a
busy, fleshy, wide-hipped body.
Just because you pretend
my arms weigh only sound,
or my voice dissolves in water
does not take me from my post—
your storefront, your parking garage,
your garden store, your library.

Hear me sing of what you're not—
nothing like bird song or slug trail,
nothing of weft or warp, nothing
that can make or create, nothing
aside from the lament of the unmade,
the forfeited, the assumed, the taken,
the dead and the many paths the dead
follow to arrive at disparate points,
at the plains of undoing. You undo
solidity, you shackle need and hope
to make them an anchor.

Each time we meet, this song catches
in my stomach, on a lung, within,
barbed into me. But I sing it now:
you are what is wrong. We all
are wrong in a pie, wrong over noodles,
wrong in an attaché, a fan belt of wrong
put back in an engine, wrong in a laptop
file or on a jump drive, ringtone wrong.
We are danger, riding high on horses
of garbage and sin, the erosion of our everyday
as it builds to a rotten letdown, to tragedy
as laziness. We are four horsepersons
of a disappointing apocalypse, our famine
is for kindness, for a hand on the arm,
for a word whispered for the sake
of that word's weight and its balm
on shattered eyes or its healing weight
in a gut yearning for sustenance. Our war
is with one another over the pale dailies,

newspaper in the shrubs, lawn too high,
the pestilence of property taxes, when
I know too many people whose hope
is tied to not being hit, or to being able
to talk to an ear that will hear. Our
war is minor, petty, a whimper. Not
now, see my roar become fire, see
voice become flame. See the scorch begin.

ACKNOWLEDGMENTS

Places where certain poems first appeared, often in slightly
different form:

Burnside Review: Granola Jones Lives Comfortably with her Inaccurate
Legends

Dislocate: Aptitude Test

Lake Effect: The Telemarketer Calls the Stevens of Hartford, Mr.
Disagreeable Wins Friends and Influences People

MAYDAY: The Television Makes Its Promise Between Channels

Mid-American Review: The Telemarketer Calls the Merwin Household,
William Watches the Telemarketer, William Notes the Boxes in
the Hall, William Gives the Gift of Sculpted Telephony

The Missouri Review: The Telemarketer Basically Enjoys Talking with
Goldbarth, Though It Ends Too Soon for Her Preference; The
Telemarketer's Husband, Unemployed, Kills Time in a Café,
Waiting to Pick Her Up; The Telemarketer Calls A Poet She's
Actually Heard Once on NPR To Talk To Him About Relief
From the Burden of High Interest Credit Cards; The Telemarketer
Means to Call Baker About Erectile Dysfunction But, in a
Misdial, Winds Up with Simic; The Telemarketer Calls Basho
about a Cure for the Winter Blues; After Calling Too Many Poets,
The Telemarketer Gives Up

Panhandler: Granola Jones' Daddy, Sweet William, Granola Jones and the Telemarketer Meet in the Hall, and Granola Jones Staggers into Knowingness at a Shelter Potluck and Fundraiser.

Porchlight: Mr. Disagreeable Embraces the Whole Bad Neighbor Thing

"Granola Jones Cooks at the Potluck," appeared in the anthology, *A Face to Meet the Faces: An Anthology of Contemporary Persona Poetry*, edited by Stacey Lynn Brown and Oliver de la Paz, 2011.

"Teleconference with Rain," appeared in my first book, *Dirt and All Its Dense Labor* (Wordtech Editions, 2006), but it fits better in this one, and is relevant to *this* story.

In "The Telemarketer Calls Basho about a Cure for the Winter Blues," the few insertions of actual Basho haiku are translations from *Basho's Haiku: Selected Poems of Matsuo Basho*, translated by David Landis Barnhill (SUNY Press, 2005).

GABRIEL WELSCH writes both fiction and poetry. Previous collections of poetry include *The Death of Flying Things* (WordTech, 2012), *Dirt and All Its Dense Labor* (WordTech, 2006) and *An Eye Fluent in Gray*, a chapbook (Seven Kitchens Press, 2010). His work has appeared in more than one hundred different journals and magazines, including *Southern Review*, *Mid-American Review*, *New Letters*, *PANK*, *Ascent*, *West Branch*, *Chautauqua*, and *The Georgia Review*. In the *Best American Short Stories 2012*, one of his stories was included in the list of "Other Distinguished Stories of 2011." He earned his MFA at Penn State and now lives in Huntingdon, Pennsylvania, with his family, and works as vice president of advancement and marketing at Juniata College and occasionally teaches writing at the Chautauqua Institution.

www.ingramcontent.com/pod-product-compliance
Lightning Source LLC
Chambersburg PA
CBHW072041040426

42447CB00012BB/2955